*Sylvain Turgeon*

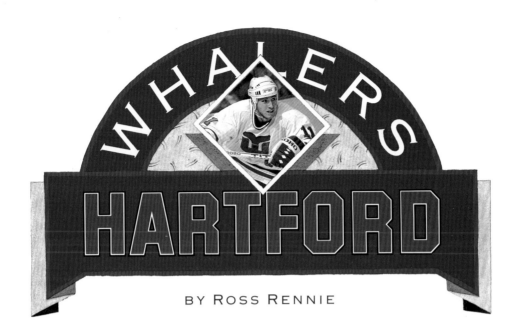

# WHALERS
# HARTFORD

BY ROSS RENNIE

CREATIVE EDUCATION INC.

Published by Creative Education, Inc.

123 S. Broad Street, Mankato, Minnesota 56001

Designed by Rita Marshall

Photos by Bruce Bennett Studios,

Frank Howard/Protography and Wide World Photos

**Library of Congress Cataloging-in-Publication Data**

Rennie, Ross.

  The Hartford Whalers/by Ross Rennie.

  p.  cm.

  Summary: Presents, in text and illustrations, the history of

the Hartford Whalers hockey team.

  ISBN 0-88682-279-3   *91-71*

  1. Hartford Whalers (Hockey team)—History—Juvenile literature.

[1. Hartford Whalers (Hockey team)—History.  2. Hockey—History.]

I. Title.

GV848.H37R46   1989

796.96'264'097463—dc20                  89-36847

                                                  CIP

                                                  AC

## THE BEGINNINGS: 1972–1976

**H**artford, Connecticut, was originally a mill town. Located on the Connecticut River, this spot in the rolling hills of northern Connecticut became the center for manufacturing in the region. As the state capital, the city has undergone a number of changes over the years. One of the original colonies, the area is also rich in early American history.

Hartford is now a high-tech and financial services center. Although the city itself is not very large, including the surrounding towns there are well over a million people who take advantage of the many attractions available in

*Ron Francis is one of the most talented Whalers of all time.*

Hartford. One of those attractions is the National Hockey League's Hartford Whaler team.

Interestingly, the Hartford Whalers hockey club did not start out in Hartford. In fact, they started out in Boston. At that time, their name was not even the Hartford Whalers but, rather, the New England Whalers. That was back in 1972, when they shared an ice rink with the Boston Bruins, the reigning Stanley Cup champions.

There were actually fourteen brand-new professional hockey teams that started their first season in 1972. The Whalers were one of those teams. It may seem unbelievable that a new team would win the league's championship cup in it's first year, but that is exactly what the Whalers did. Of course, it may be a lot more believable when you realize that the league the Whalers played in was not the NHL, but, rather, the new World Hockey Association. The cup they won was not the Stanley Cup but the AVCO World Cup, the championship trophy of the new WHA.

In 1972 the NHL was progressing along its slow path to expansion a bit at a time. It was too slow for a lot of folks who were desperate to see the exciting sport of professional hockey. Some people decided that they did not want to wait for the NHL to visit them and instead formed their own league in competition with the NHL.

The new WHA had professional teams in twelve cities that first year. It was the same year that the NHL granted franchises to two teams, the Atlanta Flames and the New York Islanders. The New England Whalers were out to prove that if New York could support two hockey teams, so could Boston.

*Rick Ley, one of the original Hartford Whalers.*

*Ted Green was named the Whalers' first team captain.*

Many folks laughed at the new league. The laughing stopped when the news broke that one of the NHL's top stars, none other than Bobby Hull, the first player to score more than fifty goals in a season, had signed a WHA contract with the Winnipeg Jets. The new league had gained instant respect.

The New England Whaler's got started on April 19, 1972, when Larry Pleau became the first player to sign a Whaler contract. Ted Green, the team's first captain, joined shortly after Pleau. Green's eight years of experience with the Stanley Cup-winning Boston Bruins gave the Whalers instant respectability.

The New England Whalers played their first game on October 12, 1972. There was a sell-out crowd of 14,442 fans on hand to see the WHA begin in Boston Garden. The Whalers played the Philadelphia Blazers that evening, and Larry Pleau, the team's first player, scored the team's first winning goal in a 4-3 Whaler victory.

Tom Webster was the scoring leader that first year with 103 points. With the solid defense provided by Rick Ley, the Whalers were a powerful force in the new league. They went on to win forty-six games that year and finish first in the East Division.

They advanced to the finals against Bobby Hull and his Winnipeg Jets. Hull, or the "Golden Jet," as he was known, was the player to stop if the team was to have a chance at victory. The Whalers strategy was just that: keep Hull off the scoring sheet. In the first game, the strategy worked. Hull was kept to one goal, and new England won 7–2. The Whalers went on to win the series to become the first ever WHA champions.

During the next six years in the WHA, the New England

Whalers would never again win the AVCO Cup, and would make only one more appearance in the play-off finals. Yet a lot of team history occurred during this period, even if play-off victories were not a part of the story.

One of the most significant changes came in 1975, when the hockey club moved from Boston to Hartford, Connecticut. The Whalers had become the "second-class" team in Boston. Hartford had pursued the team by building the Hartford Civic Center, complete with a coliseum for hockey. Opening night in the Whalers' new home occurred on January 11, 1975. In front of a sellout crowd of 10,507 fans, the Whalers defeated the San Diego Mariners 4–3 in overtime. Coach Jack Kelley was euphoric. "We should have come here (Hartford), in the first place," he said. "This is pure magic. We have found a real home in Hartford. The fans appreciate and want us." Those fans were very special, as the team was to find out a few years later.

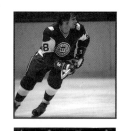

*Tom Webster led Hartford in scoring their first season with 103 points.*

## THE BIG EVENTS: 1977–1978

If 1975 was the biggest move for the franchise, 1977 marked the biggest event in the team's history. On May 23, 1977, Howard Baldwin announced the signing of Gordie Howe and his two sons, Mark and Marty. Hockey Hall of Famer Jack Adams said, "Hockey has its superstars, but it has only one superman, and that's Gordie Howe!" Superman had arrived in Hartford. Magic was in the air.

Gordie was thrilled. No other team in the WHA or NHL would have signed all three Howes following the demise of their former WHA team, the Houston Aeros. Gordie wanted to continue playing with his sons. He said of the

*Mark Howe played both defense and right wing for Hartford.*

*Brother Marty was exclusively a defenseman.*

*Gordie Howe was the inspirational leader of the Whalers.*

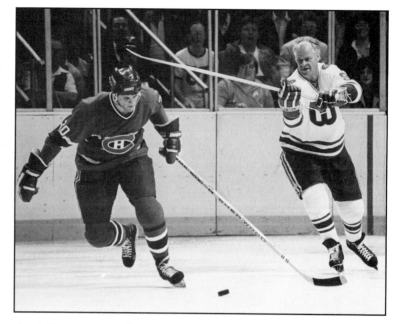

deal, "I got everything I wanted. They gave me the chance to do the thing I wanted to do. Play with my sons." Howe, true to form, did not let down his new fans. In the 1977–78 season, he led the team with ninety-six points. Not bad for a fifty-year-old grandfather in one of the toughest professional sports!

It was during that season that Gordie scored his one-thousandth professional goal. On December 7, 1977, at the Jefferson County Coliseum, Gordie Howe scored a power-play goal at 1:36 of the first period to become the only man in hockey history to reach this milestone. There were only 10,211 fans on hand to witness this great moment in hockey history.

About one month after this unique event was celebrated, Hartford faced another unique event—the loss of their home. On January 18, 1978, at 4:30 A.M., the roof of the Hartford Civic Center Coliseum collapsed due to the weight of snow and ice. Luckily, no one was killed. The New England Whalers needed a temporary home right away. The neighboring town of Springfield, Connecticut, came to the rescue. Were the fans truly loyal? The real test was now at hand.

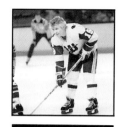

*John McKenzie and the Whalers began their last season of play in the WHL.*

The Whaler fans quickly showed their devotion to their team. The mayor of Springfield bought tickets and urged others to do the same. Season-ticket holders remained loyal: less than three hundred canceled their tickets. Within a short time, the "91 Club" was started. The club, named after the highway that joined Hartford and Springfield, was made up of stalwart Hartford fans who made the journey to Springfield for each Whaler home game.

With all the excitement over the roof collapse, it would almost be easy to overlook the fact that the Howes and Dave Keon were leading the Whalers to their second-best season ever. Some people, notably in the NHL, questioned the quality of hockey the WHA offered. The style of play was defended by Hartford's Keon. "I don't care what anyone wants to tell you . . . the fans would rather see hockey where guys make plays and where both teams have a chance to win. We have that in the WHA."

Even so, by the time the WHA started its seventh season in the fall of 1978, financial troubles had reduced the league to six teams. Talk had begun in earnest about a possible merger with the NHL.

In their final year in the WHA, the Whalers were about to set a few records of their own. Johnie "Pie" McKenzie was playing in his last season after joining the Whalers

*The legendary Gordie Howe was Hartford's leading scorer.*

from the Boston Bruins in 1977. It was McKenzie's efforts as a player that helped attract fans and keep them loyal. And, it was due in large part to fan support that this team would be one of only four WHA teams to survive long enough to join the NHL in 1979. Before doing so, they set a professional hockey record for distance traveled during a play-off series. They amassed a total of 14,568 air miles.

In the semifinal play-off series, Hartford met the Edmonton Oilers, a hockey club from 2,428 miles away. The series went to the seventh game, requiring Hartford to cover the distance six times to set the record. Beyond the travel, the series was an exciting one. In the first two games in Edmonton, the Oiler forwards Wayne Gretzky, Blair MacDonald, and Brett Callighen had a field day. Edmonton rolled to two straight victories. When play resumed in Springfield, the Whalers shifted to a defensive style. In the third game, the Oilers made only twenty-three shots on goal, and the Whalers won 3–1. The teams traded victories in the next two games.

Now, with nearly ten thousand miles already traveled, the Whalers returned to their home rink in Springfield. Each team had won every game on their home ice. Game six was no exception. Almost everyone on the team contributed to the 8–4 victory—a victory that meant another trip to Edmonton. The final game of the series, just like those before it, went to the home team. With a 6–3 victory, Edmonton won a trip to the last WHA play-off finals against the Winnipeg Jets. The Jets, behind the power of Bobby Hull, went on to win the final WHA AVCO Cup.

The traveling record was not the only one the Whalers set in 1979. Mark Howe set his own personal record by scoring 107 points. Not bad considering that Mark was a

defenseman. The comparisons with Bobby Orr began. Mark Howe was starting to move out of the shadow of his father, said to be hockey's greatest player.

## THE MOVE TO THE NHL: 1979–1980

In the spring of 1979, negotiations were being completed that would spell the end of the WHA and result in four new teams being added to the NHL. The Whalers knew they would be one of the lucky original WHA teams to join the NHL. They also knew that Hartford would be their permanent home. The fans were proving their loyalty

*Dave Keon (above) and Mike Rogers (right) were key players in Hartford's first season in the NHL.*

*Mark Howe led the Whaler defense in 1980.*

*John McKenzie's spirited play led the Whalers into the NHL.*

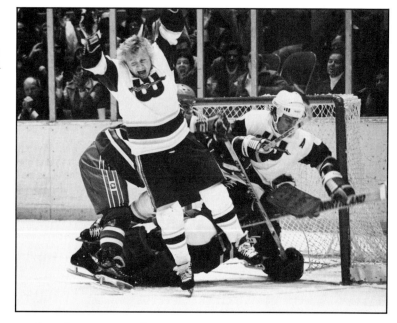

under the worst of situations. So, on May 23, 1979, the team announced their name would be changed to the Hartford Whalers. The Whalers would start a new chapter of their club history with a new name.

As if to preserve the team's WHA heritage, the Whalers retired their first player number. It was John McKenzie's number 19. McKenzie had played for the team for only two seasons, but his "never-say-die" attitude had inspired the team and helped build critical fan support. During his two years, he had scored fifty-seven goals, many of them game winners. With McKenzie's number retired, Hartford would start their NHL years with some definite history.

That first NHL season was notable in many respects. Hartford started their season on October 11, 1979, when they met the Minnesota North Stars. Unfortunately, Minnesota did not give Hartford a warm welcome, defeating the Whalers 4-1. About a week later, on October 19, 1979, Hartford recorded their first NHL win. In a 6-3 victory over the Los Angeles Kings, both Marty and Gordie Howe contributed to the Whalers' scoring. Gordie Howe was once again in the NHL, and fans all over North America came to see hockey's superman.

*Bobby Hull and Gordie Howe, two of hockey's immortals, were teammates for nine games.*

As if one big-name player was not enough, when the Winnipeg Jets were having problems coming to contract terms with Bobby Hull, Hartford made him an offer. Although specific contract terms were not finalized, Hull made the move to the Whalers. It was the only time that two of the NHL's greatest stars, Howe and Hull, played on the same team. Bobby Hull never did come to a contract agreement with Hartford, and after only nine games with the team he officially retired. Hull, who had given the WHA the credibility it needed when it was organized in 1972, did not successfully make the move back to the NHL. Both Bobby Hull and Gordie Howe were known as gentlemen. They both had one other thing in common. Both famous players wore the number 9. When Hull joined Hartford, Gordie Howe had already claimed that number. During the few games the two men played together, Hull wore the number 16, the only time in his hockey career he had not worn the number he made famous.

During that first season, perhaps the biggest event was the team's move back home to Hartford, after an absence of over two years. During that time, the team had changed its name and changed leagues. There was a lot of excitement that first season in the NHL. Blaine "Stash" Stoughton scored fifty-six goals for Hartford that year. Stoughton's forty-four assists gave him 100 points; Mike Rogers ended the year with 105 points. This would be the only season

that Hartford had two 100-plus point scorers on the team. Blaine Stoughton was one of only two players to score fifty or more goals in a season in both the WHA and the NHL. The only other player to accomplish this feat was Bobby Hull.

With only twenty-seven wins that first season, Hartford finished fourth in the Norris Division and qualified for the play-offs. That was the good news. The bad news was that Hartford's opponents in the first round would be the powerful Montreal Canadiens, who had won the Stanley Cup for the past four years. The best-of-five-games series was over in three quick games. Hartford would play seven seasons in the NHL before winning their first play-off game.

Even though Montreal won all three play-off games, the series will go down in Hartford and NHL history. It was during this series that Gordie Howe got his last NHL play-off goal and assist. Howe retired after that season. In his thirty-two seasons as a professional hockey player in both the WHA and the NHL, he had become the all-time leader in many hockey categories. His thirty-two seasons (twenty-six in the NHL) were a record in themselves. During those seasons, he played in 2,421 games, another record. He set another record in scoring, with 1,071 goals, 1,518 assists, and a total of 2,589 points.

There is one other record that Gordie Howe owns: he is the only NHL player to have his number retired in two buildings. He was accorded this honor in the Detroit Red Wings' arena as well as the Hartford Whalers' arena. After retiring as a player, Gordie remained active in the NHL by taking an administrative post in the Whaler organization.

1 9 8 0

*Gordie Howe retired as hockey's all-time scoring leader with 2,589 points.*

*After Gordie Howe's retirement, players like Blaine Stoughton got their opportunity with the Whalers.*

## TODAY'S HARTFORD WHALERS:
## THE 1980s AND BEYOND

*Larry Pleau was one of three different head coaches to lead the Whalers in one year.*

Following a very exciting and eventful first year in the NHL, the Hartford Whalers went into a period of rebuilding. Even though they were a new team in a new league, they had been around for eight years. There were many older players on the team who needed to be replaced if Hartford was to be a contender in the NHL. The changes that were needed took a long time. It would be six years before the Whalers would win more than thirty games in a season, and the same six years before they would get another opportunity to participate in the Stanley Cup play-offs.

Many changes occurred during this time, not the least of which was a variety of coaches. After what appeared to be "coach of the month" for the first three years, the Whalers hired Jack Evans. Evans led the team from September 1983 until February 1988. At that point, with the team in a slump, Evans was replaced by Larry Pleau, the first player signed by the New England Whalers back in 1972. As a player, he had helped form part of the Whaler history. As a coach, his task was to create some Whaler play-off history.

The Whalers shifted NHL divisions in 1981. As a part of the final realignment of teams, they shifted from the Norris Division to the tough Adams Division. The Adams Division was made up of teams from the Northeast: Boston, Montreal, Quebec, Buffalo, and Hartford. Also, the unbalanced schedule was adopted. This type of schedule meant that teams within a division played each other twice as often during the regular season as they played other NHL teams.

Going to battle often with strong teams like Montreal and Boston made life tough for Hartford during the early 1980s. For the first four years in their new division, they ended up in last place and out of the play-offs.

In order to help accomplish the difficult task of rebuilding a championship team, the Whalers hired Emile Francis in 1983. "The Cat," as Francis was nicknamed, was known for his uncanny ability to pounce on opportunities to make trades and acquire talent needed to build a winner. At about the same time, another fellow by the name of Francis joined Hartford. Ron Francis was no relation to Emile but, in fact, was a second cousin to Hartford goaltender Mike Liut.

*Goaltender Mike Liut joined Hartford and was instrumental in the team's improvement.*

Ron Francis was to establish many team records over the next few years, as well as lead his team in scoring four times. Ron would eventually hold the most individual team records, including most games, most goals, most assists, most points, and most consecutive twenty-goal seasons. Ron was also one of only two players to score more than five hundred points while a Whaler. The other player to accomplish this feat was John Anderson. Ron's efforts would lead to his being named team captain in 1985. He was a key member of the Whalers' community relations program and in 1986 won the Whalers' Founders Trophy for outstanding community work. Ron Francis and his second cousin Mike Liut would play very important roles in the rebirth of the Whaler hockey club.

While new ground was being broken in the Hartford franchise, old achievements were being recognized. The third Hartford player jersey was retired. Rick Ley had joined the New England Whalers back in 1972. He was a defensive star in the WHA, a league that did not have many

*Right winger John Anderson was acquired in a trade with Quebec in 1986.*
*(pages 26–27)*

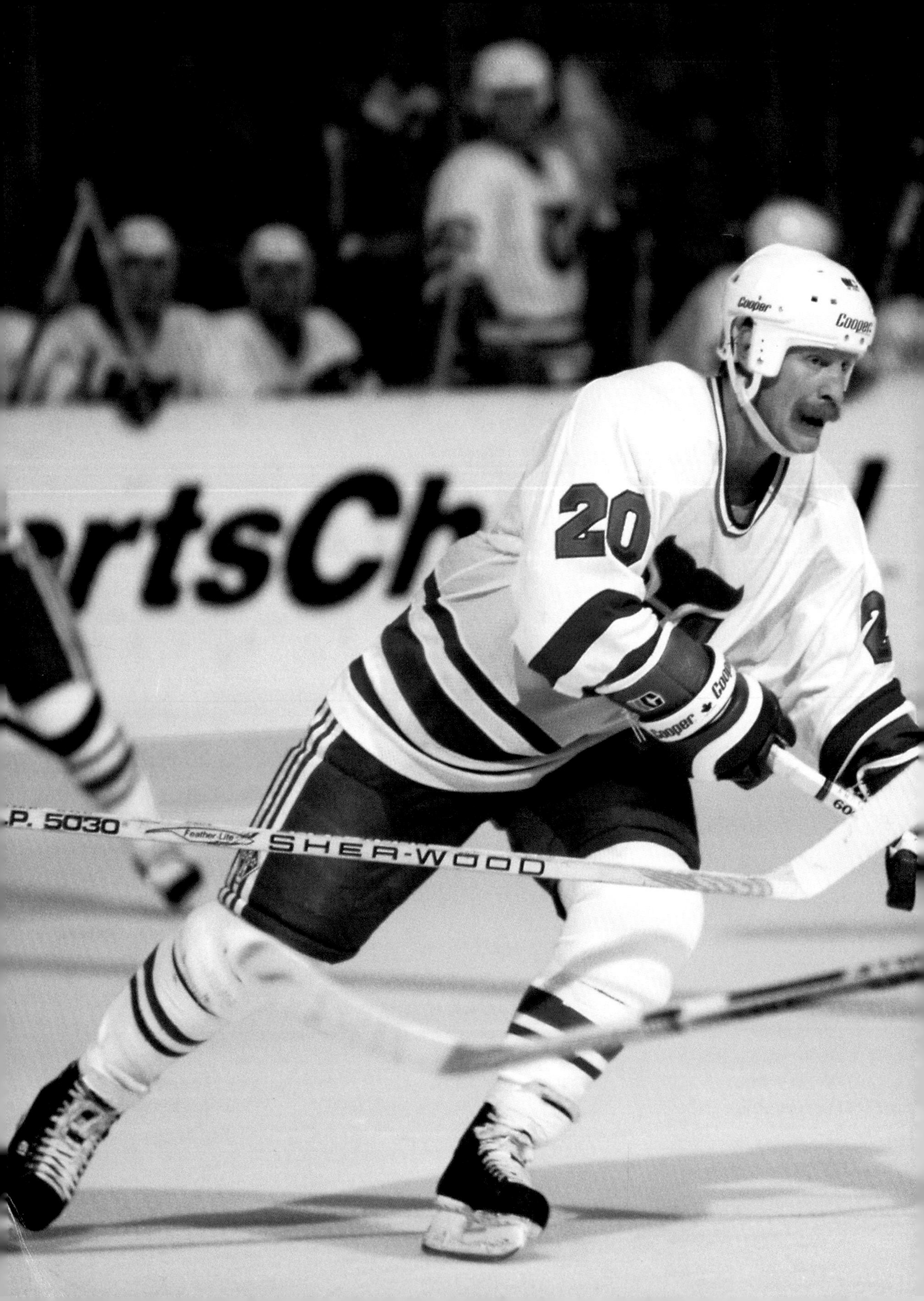
Cooper
20
P. 5030
Feather Lite
SHER-WOOD

*Dave Babych led Hartford to the play-offs for the first time in eight years.*

great defenseman. His efforts did not go unnoticed. Ley was selected for and played in every WHA All-Star game. It was both talent and personality that got him selected as captain of the Whalers in 1975, a position he would hold for six years. Rick Ley's number 2 was the third Whaler jersey to be hoisted to the rafters of the Hartford Coliseum beside those of Gordie Howe and John McKenzie.

With history recorded, new blood in the form of youth and talent was being gathered together. Mike Liut joined Hartford in 1985 when "the Cat" obtained him from the St. Louis Blues. Mike was to make an immediate impact on the team's results. In the 1985–86 season, the team earned its first trip to post-season play since 1980.

To see how tough life was in the Adams Division, one need only look at the 1986 final standings. For starters, Hartford earned the last play-off spot on the final night of the regular season by beating the Toronto Maple Leafs 7-1. First place that year went to the Quebec Nordiques with ninety-two points. Last place went to the Buffalo Sabres with eighty points. Only eight points separated the four teams that qualified for the play-offs.

After waiting six years to pursue the Stanley Cup, Hartford was ready to give each game their all. Their first opponents were the Quebec Nordiques. The series was typical of two very closely matched teams. Hartford won three straight games behind the outstanding goaltending of Mike Liut, who provided the Whalers with both leadership and solid defense. "Liut's the cornerstone of the Whalers," said Emile Francis. "He gives us the stability that no other goalie could give us."

*Mike Liut led the Whalers' drive to the play-offs.*     29

*Along with Liut, center Dave Tippett provided solid play.*

*Sylvain Turgeon gave the Whalers much needed offensive support.*     31

*Carey Wilson was obtained from Calgary in exchange for Dana Murzyn and Shane Churla.*

Hartford faced the Montreal Canadiens next. The series would truly be a goaltenders' duel between Mike Liut and rookie Montreal goaltender Patrick Roy.

Hartford extended the series to seven games before Montreal prevailed in the deciding contest. No team that gives the type of effort that Hartford did takes any joy in losing. The Whalers, in reflection, had come the closest of any team to beating the 1986 Stanley Cup champions, the Montreal Canadiens. Patrick Roy, who had frustrated the Hartford team, went on to win the Conn Smythe Trophy as the most valuable player in the play-offs.

Many teams, following hard-fought play-off defeats, do not perform well during the next regular season. Hartford did the reverse. They finished the 1986–87 season in first place in the Adams Division with ninety-three points. The team could display their first NHL banner as regular-season leader in their division. Unfortunately, like the regular season, the Adams Division play-offs were always tough to win. The Quebec Nordiques would turn the tables on Hartford from the previous season. In a high-scoring series, Quebec sent the favored Whalers on summer vacation after only six games.

The following year Hartford faced Montreal in the play-offs and lost three games by one goal to end their play-off hopes early. Hartford's play-off success would, for a long time, be hampered by the difficulty in winning the Adams Division title.

The Hartford Whalers, with a rich history, loyal fans, and an AVCO championship to their record, will certainly one day again be champions. And next time it will be the Stanley Cup championship.